purple heart:

say what you mean, and mean what you say

words by Rodnika Connor

a dedication to all that reads this.....

and my beautiful family....

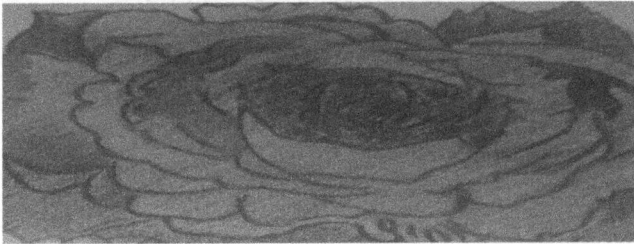

Artwork by Devon Reynolds

one

they say all good things eventually come to an end

but with you my heart beats like life just begin

trying to figure out how one person can have so

much control over my heart

but some things you don't have an answer to

just hoping that we never part

love can bring pain and sometimes pain brings love

I'm willing to sacrifice that because I know you're the one

if your plans are different from mines please tell me now

because I don't think I can take

another let down

time tells all things, with patience
comes strength

I'm willing to wait for love

I just hope you stay around until then

two

*Fighting temptation is the one thing
that always seems to fail*

*and wanting something so bad feels
like heaven right before it turns into
hell*

*yes the bad will certainly follow the
good*

*I learned when you follow your heart
you start to do things you probably
never should*

*what's happiness today if tomorrow is
only going to bring you pain*

*now I get why people live in the
moment*

*because worrying takes the joy out of
things*

you ask me what I want

and of course the answer is going to

be you

but is this worth going after

tell me that you'll sacrifice too

we know that nothing is promised to us later

and I don't want to feel like I gave in

I keep opening this door of temptation

should have known from the beginning I wouldn't win

three

Morning blues

*these are the moments that I wish
you were the one I could wake up
next to*

*right now, you are nothing but a
fantasy*

*so I'll keep dreaming until the day you
become my reality*

give me one wish

and I'll guarantee it's to have you

*the control that you have over my
mind*

there's really nothing I can do

what will it take to have you around

from the morning I wake up

or at night when the sun goes down

these lonely mornings sometimes
make me feel weak

I'm trying to find happiness

loving you, my heart will be at peace

four

give me diamonds

give me gold

maybe even money

but all of those things are worthless

if you're not here to love me

life without you

is like heaven without its angels

like a lost child in the park

with no one around to save you

you see

I can't imagine trying to love anyone else

your smile is my heartbeat

I would be crazy to give that up

I'm so far gone

right now would be too late to stop

all the material things in the world

are no competition to what we've got

five

she told me don't worry about a thing

that I would always be taken care of

things I didn't know then that I know now

I owe the thanks to my first love

the first to ever nurture me

and show me the way of life

from seeing me through dark times

to tucking me in at night

God is the center of all things

but there's nothing like a mother

all these years later

and I'm still trying to find ways to thank her

six

she's my life

and my other half

probably know me more than i know myself..

no matter how many times we had an argument

when I called

she didn't hesitate to help

a sister is a friend

that will last through your entire life time

while everyone else comes and go

nothing will ever break

that beautiful bond

if I knew then

that you looked up to me

I probably would have reconsidered

did things differently

but then I realized

you were never judging

you just managed to find the good in me

being that I'm older

you may think

I always know what to do

but the truth is you're my hero

and now, I look up to you

seven

your face is the reason that I smile

I look at you

and began to feel weak

hoping it's you

when I hear my phone ring

I wish that you knew

how fast my heart beat

I'm not sure if this is love

*but it feels something like it when
you're here*

it's like

*I'm suffocating when you're not
around me*

the only way to save me

is by breathing your air

in too deep

I have no one to blame but you

you've put a spell on me permanently

and nothing else matters but you

is this love

maybe it's just infatuation

time tells everything

tell me you'll be more

than just an imagination

eight

do I deserve to be loved

that's a question I ask myself from time to time

but only when I sit and think

about the mistakes I've made

and guilt starts taking control of my mind

I'll ask for forgiveness

just to do the same things

I've done a million times before

just want to get it right this time

can't take feeling ashamed anymore

sadness, lonely days

and going to sleep with so many regrets

or convincing myself

that a person like me

should probably deserve less

yes I know I'm human

and its moments where we mess up

but I've been given so many chances

at times I feel like giving up

if you could listen to my thoughts

you would hear me say

that I'll be alone forever

but I know the past doesn't control the future

even I deserve a happily ever after

nine

I've watched the happiness train go by so many times

never knew how sad I was

didn't realize that I was living a lie

it became so normal to smile

because I knew everyone was watching me

if only they could see my pain

but, I'd rather hide that part of me

one day, I'm going to open my eyes

and the darkness will be gone

I'll learn how to take control

and let all negative things go

I'm ready to board the train of happiness

no more letting it pass me by

this time around

you'll see the real me

*the person that's leaving the past
behind*

ten

Growing up

I thought I would never want to leave
my city

so much fun as a kid

I was proud to say

"I'm from philly"

but then you realize

things aren't really the same
anymore

those childhood memories fade

and you suddenly feel you want more

more than a guy

whose calling your name as you walk
by

or the newest shoes

to finally "look better than your

friends this time"

see sometimes as you grow

many things out grow you....

and your goals in life

*should be the only competition that
you look forward to*

loving one place for so long

can eventually become old

I'm on a new path for right now

but all of those beautiful memories

my heart will forever hold

eleven

night time

I usually call it my time

seems like that's when I can be myself

relax, unwind, and let my hair down

now I can finally cater to myself

I admit

things are always fun

when you're right here with me

but this time alone

is certainly what I've been missing

as I explore my body

my guilty mind seems to shift to you

but truthfully

when it comes to a woman loving herself

we know exactly what to do

there used to be a time

when I would feel so ashamed

but baby you have no worries

because as I climax

I'll be screaming your name

twelve

he gave me the green light

told me that it was my world

honestly I knew this moment would come

it was meant for me to be your girl

I want to be the last person you speak to

before you go to bed at night

and when we finally make love

I know it's going to be one crazy ride

you see, I've been dreaming of this day

for such a long time

but I knew you weren't quite ready

to finally become mine

now that you're here

I've been nothing but smiles

whatever it is you're doing to me

I could get used to it for a while

my pride went out the window

and all that's left is my heart

it feels so amazing to know with you

I finally let down my guard

thirteen

if I had to survive off of love

I wonder how long would I live

I'm hoping forever

because I can't get enough

of everything you give

from the way you touch me

and whisper sweet nothings in my ear

I'm constantly on cloud nine

every single minute that you're here

how does one come down

from a love so amazingly high

i look at you and see something more beautiful

than heaven and it's blue skies

if I had to survive off of love

it would only be love from you

enough to live a lifetime

as long as it's a life spent with you

fourteen

I've met many people in my lifetime

yet I haven't met you

*they say all good things are worth
waiting for*

and I've been searching for you

high and low

through happiness and pain

being alone all these years

things really have to change

it's easy to fall for someone

just to past the time

but I'm anticipating the moment

when your heart becomes mine

I know you're somewhere out there

hoping to find me too

some days you seem so far

it's like I'm never going to find you

but true love equals patience

and with patience comes strength

the day that we finally meet

my life will feel complete again

fifteen

it's someone for everyone

but what if that someone that I want
is you

some say you're out of my league

and now I have something to prove

that a girl like me

can have whatever she wants

if she just puts her mind to it

I'm up for the challenge of making
you mines

and I'm not ashamed to show it

only a real man would recognize a
queen

and a real woman would see that he's
a king

if you decide give me you

*I promise you won't ever regret a
thing*

you see you've got me open

to the point that I'm so far gone

I wake up to the thought of you

especially moments when I'm alone

what will it take

*for me to have such a beautiful
creation of a guy like you*

it would take for you to realize

that I am just as beautiful too

sixteen

he calls me his good girl

but what if I want to be bad

acting out my fantasies is my fear

but I just want something I've never had

he calls me his good girl

and I don't want to let him down

if he knew all of my thoughts

I doubt that he would still be around

this love thing is so crazy

it just leaves me feeling confused

but he calls me his good girl

and now I have to choose

to listen to my heart

and behave myself like I always do

or give in to my mind

telling me that I need someone else to
pleasure me too

you see to satisfy my body

it'll take more than one man

but he calls me his good girl

if i told him the truth

he just wouldn't understand

seventeen

while you're over there enjoying life

I'm here picking up pieces

I thought that I was over you

this isn't the way I pictured it

why was it so easy to fall

yet so hard to let go

I wish that I had never met you

then maybe I could get back my soul

is this what heartbreak feels like?

as if I have nothing else to live for

or feeling empty inside

I swear my heart can't take this anymore

tell me this is all a nightmare

and that you want me back in your

life

am I really that desperate

*that I would settle for more of your
hurt pain and lies*

some would say

maybe I don't realize my own worth

but I really had no idea

how bad this love thing hurt

maybe when tomorrow comes

I can work on loving me

but tonight the only thing that I want

*is to have the one thing that's bad for
me*

eighteen

tomorrow isn't promised to any of us

so why not just live for today

I've spend many nights

feeling regret for so many things

not realizing the days are just fading away

they say there's no greater moment

than the one you're living in right now

but I admit it's hard at times

especially when I begin to think

that I've let myself down

yes I'm human

and sometimes we don't always get things right

imperfections are what makes us perfect

and that's the best part of life

the past is exactly that

*something that could stand in the
way of the future*

so I'll choose to live for today,

and look forward to becoming better

nineteen

tonight I'll be all you want me to be

but tell me will that be enough

you say that it's hard for me to be submissive

tell me that a pretty girl shouldn't be so tough

so tonight, I'll try something different

maybe I'll change your mind

allow you to see a different me

and maybe you'll be satisfied this time

lately I'm questioning things

like maybe what I've been doing isn't enough

but then again, I should be questioning you

what's wrong with being myself?

the woman you fell in love with

and wanted to give the world

does it mean if I don't change for you

that you'll leave me for another girl

will it be a lost for me

most likely a loss for you

tonight I'll be what you want me to be

*but it doesn't mean I'm giving in to
you*

twenty

you say you need a good woman

but are you a good man

when I say good

I don't mean perfect

*but you have to represent the same
things that you ask*

*like for me to be loving, faithful, loyal
and trustworthy*

this isn't a one sided deal

just like you it has to benefit me

I love simple things

*especially things that money can't
buy*

I know you've heard it all before

but the real proof is in the heart

and the heart never lies

commitment is a challenge for me

I'm sure it's the same for you too

but love is the ultimate goal

and can't wait to be the one to give that to you

you ask me am I ready to be your good woman

yes if you're ready to be my good man

just give me exactly what I give to you

that's the only way this love will last

twenty-one

give me what you owe me

but that would probably take a
lifetime

why is it that when you give someone
your heart and soul

you also start to lose a piece of your
mind

is it even possible

to live inside a body and you're not
the one that's in control

the moment I fell under your spell

 I may as well just given you my entire
soul

 it may sound crazy

but this is the only way I could explain
the damage that you've done

I don't think I can ever fall in love

again

I guess this is the part where i tell you

that I give up and you've won

you got exactly what you wanted

did what you wanted to do

*and that's leaving me with nothing
but heartbreak*

while trying to get over you

the only thing I want

*is to get back my happiness and
peace*

*that's what you owe me, can I have it
back please*

twenty-two

as I get ready to walk down the aisle

I'm hoping to not have change of
heart

they say this is every girls' dream

but now that this moment is close

I somehow wish it was far

if you asked me yesterday

I would tell you I'm ready a thousand
times

but today I'm not so sure of this love

I probably shouldn't be listening to
my mind

I know it's wrong to think about it
now

while my future is waiting on the
other end of the door

*contemplating making the nearest
exit*

*to avoid telling him I'm not in love
anymore*

there it is I said it

and it feels like a part of me just died

*but the only thing that's worse than
that*

*is allowing myself to continue to live a
lie*

you didn't realize I was hurting

*I should have been honest and told
you*

that I'm in love with someone else

*and that's the reason why I can't
marry you*

Thank you so much for reading, until next time

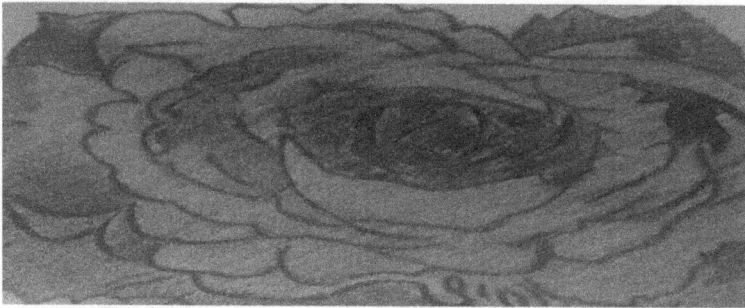

Love, Rodnika